AFRICAN AMERICAN LEADERS OF COURAGE

SOJOURNER TRUTH

KRISTEN SUSIENKA

PowerKiDS press™

New York

Published in 2020 by The Rosen Publishing Group, Inc.
29 East 21st Street, New York, NY 10010

First Edition

Editor: Kristen Susienka
Book Design: Michael Flynn

Photo Credits: Cover, pp. 1, 11 Bettmann/Getty Images; series background Kharchenko Rusian/Shutterstock.com; p. 5 https://en.wikipedia.org/wiki/Sojourner_Truth#/media/File:Sojourner_Truth,_1870.tif; pp. 7, 13 (all), 19 Everett Historical/Shutterstock.com; p. 9 Hulton Archive/Getty Images; p. 15 MPI/Archive Photos/Getty Images; p. 17 Afro Newspaper/Gado/Archive Photos/Getty Images; p. 21 Jeff Greenberg/Universal Images Group/Getty Images.

Library of Congress Cataloging-in-Publication Data

Names: Susienka, Kristen, author.
Title: Sojourner Truth / Kristen Susienka.
Description: New York : PowerKids Press, [2020] | Series: African American
  leaders of courage | Includes index.
Identifiers: LCCN 2019011987| ISBN 9781725308503 (pbk.) | ISBN 9781725308527
  (library bound) | ISBN 9781725308510 (6 pack)
Subjects: LCSH: Truth, Sojourner, 1799-1883–Juvenile literature. | African
  American abolitionists–Biography–Juvenile literature. | African American
  women–Biography–Juvenile literature. | Abolitionists–United
  States–Biography–Juvenile literature. | Social reformers–United
  States–Biography–Juvenile literature.
Classification: LCC E185.97.T8 S87 2020 | DDC 326/.8092 [B] –dc23
LC record available at https://lccn.loc.gov/2019011987

Manufactured in the United States of America

CPSIA Compliance Information: Batch #CWPK20. For Further Information contact Rosen Publishing, New York, New York at 1-800-237-9932.

CONTENTS

A Powerful Speaker

Sojourner Truth was an important woman in the 1800s. She was born a **slave** around 1797 and grew up in New York. As an adult, she was a powerful speaker for the **abolitionist** and women's rights movements.

5

Growing Up in New York

Sojourner's birth name was Isabella Baumfree. She grew up speaking Dutch. She was forced to work for many families. Her masters beat her a lot. She had five children while she was a slave. In 1826, she escaped to **freedom** with her youngest child.

7

Keeping Family Together

Isabella fought for the return of her son, Peter. He'd been sold into slavery in Alabama. Peter was returned to Isabella after she won a court case. After this, she moved to New York City with her two youngest children.

9

Religious Calling

Since childhood, Isabella had many dreams. Sometimes she heard voices. She thought God was talking to her. So, Isabella became a **preacher**. She felt called to tell the truth, so she renamed herself Sojourner Truth. Soon after, she moved to Massachusetts.

Traveling the United States

Sojourner Truth was a good speaker. People liked the way she spoke and what she said. Abolitionists Frederick Douglass and William Lloyd Garrison noticed her. They suggested that Sojourner travel the United States to speak about ending slavery.

Frederick Douglass

William Lloyd Garrison

13

Writing Her Story

Although she was a skilled speaker, Sojourner never learned to read or write. In 1850, she told her life story to Olive Gilbert. Olive wrote Sojourner's words into an **autobiography**.
The book sold very well. Sojourner bought a house with the money she made from her book's sales.

SOJOURNER TRUTH.

NARRATIVE

OF

SOJOURNER TRUTH,

A

NORTHERN SLAVE,

EMANCIPATED FROM BODILY SERVITUDE BY THE STATE OF
NEW YORK, IN 1828.

WITH A PORTRAIT.

'SWEET is the virgin honey, though the wild bee store it in a reed;
And bright the jewelled band that circleth an Ethiop's arm;
Pure are the grains of gold in the turbid stream of the Ganges;
And fair the living flowers that spring from the dull cold sod.
Wherefore, thou gentle student, ber'd thine ear to my speech,
For I also am as thou art; our hearts can commune together:
To meanest matters will I stoop, for mean is the lot of mortal;
I will rise to noblest themes, for the soul hath a heritage of glory.'

BOSTON:
PRINTED FOR THE AUTHOR.
1850.

A Mighty Speech

In 1851, Sojourner gave her most famous speech. This was at a women's rights event in Ohio. She spoke in support of rights for women. She pointed out that she was a woman, too. This speech is often called "Ain't I a Woman?"

17

During and After the Civil War

The American Civil War took place from 1861 to 1865. Sojourner helped by sending supplies to black soldiers in the **Union** army. In 1864, she visited the White House. After the war, she **counseled** newly freed slaves and worked for women's rights.

Sojourner's Spirit Lives On

Sojourner Truth lived the rest of her life in Battle Creek, Michigan. She died there in 1883. People remember her for her bravery and her speeches. There are many statues of her and stories about her. Her spirit lives on today.

21

THE LIFE OF SOJOURNER TRUTH

1797 — Sojourner Truth is born Isabella Baumfree.

1826 — Isabella escapes to freedom.

1843 — Isabella changes her name to Sojourner Truth.

1851 — Sojourner Truth gives her most famous speech.

1883 — Sojourner Truth dies.

GLOSSARY

abolitionist: Someone who fights to end slavery.

autobiography: A book that tells the story of a person's life that is written by the person it is about.

counsel: To give advice to someone.

freedom: The state of being free.

preacher: A religious speaker.

slave: A person "owned" by another person and forced to work without pay.

Union: The side of the Northern states in the American Civil War.

INDEX

WEBSITES

Due to the changing nature of Internet links, PowerKids Press has developed an online list of websites related to the subject of this book. This site is updated regularly. Please use this link to access the list: www.powerkidslinks.com/AALC/truth